Paper Pom-Poms

20 CREATIVE PROJECTS TO DECORATE YOUR LIFE

Paula Pascual

LARK
New York

An Imprint of Sterling Publishing Co., Inc.
1166 Avenue of the Americas
New York, NY 10036

First published in the United Kingdom in
2016 by Carlton Books Ltd

© 2016 by Carlton Publishing Group

ISBN 978-1-4547-0908-4

For information about custom editions,
special sales, and premium and
corporate purchases, please contact
Sterling Special Sales at 800-805-5489
or specialsales@sterlingpublishing.com.

Manufactured in China

2 4 6 8 10 9 7 5 3 1

www.sterlingpublishing.com
www.larkcrafts.com

CONTENTS

Introduction 4

Tools and Materials 5

Basic Tool Kit 6

THE PROJECTS 8

Simple Paper Pom-Pom 10

Gift Box Topper 14

Ice-cream Cone 18

Fairy Lights 22

House Plant 26

Bridal Bouquet 30

Brooch/Boutonnière 34

Doily Decoration 38

Flower Table Decorations 42

Tassel Garland 46

Crepe Paper Flowers 50

Butterfly 54

Honeycomb Pom-Pom 58

Snowman 62

Heart Keepsake 66

Easter Banner 70

Pumpkin 74

Festive Ornament 78

Gift Wrapping 82

Christmas Wreath 86

Templates 90

Acknowledgments 96

INTRODUCTION

Growing up as the daughter of a fine artist exposed me to beautiful papers, paints and, more importantly, art. The pity was that I could not (and still can't) draw! But, the allure of creativity and paper never left me and slowly developed over time. I began using dried flowers and leaves to create home decorations, which soon led to playing around with gorgeous papers and making cards. My love of paper-crafting continued through my teens as a hobby and when I moved to England from Mallorca in my early twenties, I started selling my handmade cards. This led me to start teaching how to make them, and from then on I have been working in the paper-craft industry with all types of jobs, from workshop teacher, demonstrator, designer for craft magazines to craft product design.

I love color. I am a visual person and I find that it truly has the ability to lift my spirits. I also enjoy looking at extravagant shop window displays and leafing through interior design magazines – spending hours looking at beautiful things always inspires me. That inspiration always leads somewhere – it may not turn out to be what I first had in mind, but the process of exploring the creative possibilities is an exciting one. I believe this is the most important part of my creative process – it's when the best ideas, techniques and color combinations spark into life. That is the fun of creativity – disconnecting with your busy day-to-day life and letting your hands get busy instead.

Paper is a medium that works well for so many different things and paper-crafting is quick and easy to learn. One of the joys of working with paper is that it is inexpensive and readily available, and tissue paper is no exception. Working with it has some challenges, as it's very delicate and can be torn easily, but if you're gentle and handle it with care, you can create some exquisite results.

Paper pom-poms are fun and displaying them brings color and detail, a party atmosphere, or sophisticated handmade décor to a room. The possibilities are endless – change color, sizes, mix-and-match techniques from different projects – there is so much you can do with a bit of tissue paper, wire, and ribbon!

Making a pom-pom is not an exact science and that is part of the charm – no two will be identical. However, as a rough guide, the length of the short side of the paper you start with will be the approximate diameter of the finished pom-pom. You'll discover that measurements are given for each project in this book but all sizes are approximate. You'll also find tips and ideas for variations among the individual projects, so go ahead, have fun and experiment. Many of the projects in this book started their life looking very different from the end result. That is why I love paper-crafting, it's such a creative journey – you never know the destination but you always know that you will have fun!

TOOLS AND MATERIALS

You may find that you already have some of these items in your home, but if not, you can source them at most craft-supply stores.

Papers The quality of tissue paper can vary, but not so much that it will make a difference when making pom-poms. Most patterned tissue paper is more brittle than plain paper, which means it will be more challenging to separate the layers of your pom-pom without tearing the paper, so be sure to consider that when choosing which paper to use. You will also need crepe paper for some of the projects in the book. This also comes in many different qualities – I prefer the thick luxurious variety, as it is easier to work with and keeps its shape better.

Cupcake/muffin liners and doilies You may already have these in your kitchen cupboards! If not, you can find them in most supermarkets and cooking stores.

Rotary cutter and quilter's ruler Using a handheld rotary cutter against a ruler (either acrylic or metal) is the best way to cut several layers of tissue paper accurately.

Self-healing cutting mat You will need a large mat to cut against when using a rotary cutter. This is also a useful tool when using a hot glue gun.

Scissors A very strong pair of scissors that will cut many layers of tissue paper and thin wire is an essential tool.

Hot glue gun This is the most effective method for attaching bulky pom-poms to each other for a quick, strong bond. I recommend using the cool melt version (which is still pretty hot!) – the lower temperature allows the glue to cool down quicker and so the items bond together faster. However, the hotter guns will ultimately be slightly stronger in terms of bonding items together. You'll need to invest in many glue refills, as well.

Tacky craft glue This tacky, white glue is very useful for more detailed work. I always decant the glue into a smaller bottle with a fine nozzle, so that very small amounts of glue can be applied at a time.

Craft wire For the projects in this book, I mostly used 26-gauge craft wire, but it is best to increase the thickness of the wire for larger pom-poms, and for the Crepe Paper Flowers (see pages 50–53).

Ribbon or twine Building up a stash of ribbons or twine in a range of colours and thicknesses will serve you well to hang your pom-poms.

Fine craft tweezers Both straight and reverse styled tweezers are always useful when doing intricate paper-craft work.

Small stapler This is a very useful tool to attach ribbon and twine to pom-poms when you need something stronger than regular adhesives.

Pencil You'll need a standard pencil for marking out measurements and glue lines.

Paper brads These stationery items are useful for holding pom-pom layers together at the center.

Stiletto This handy tool can be used for many areas of crafting, including sewing. Here it's useful as a sharp tool to pin layers of paper.

Embossing tool This tool will help you to effortlessly crease and fold your paper and cardstock to achieve a professional finish.

Floral tape, pipe cleaners, and polystyrene shapes These are all used in some of the projects.

Polystyrene balls These are the ideal base for many craft activities. They come in many sizes and are available from most craft stores.

Die cutting machine This tool is not essential, as you can make all of the projects in this book by hand. However, if you're considering making this investment for your paper-crafting, it is incredibly useful. This machine, along with the metal dies, will be truly time-saving. You can create identical circles with ease and die-cut more than two layers of regular paper at once. There are many different sizes and different manufacturers, so you can find them at a price point to suit you.

BASIC TOOL KIT

1   Papers

2   Cupcake/Muffin liners and doilies

3   Rotary cutter

4   Self-healing cutting mat

5   Scissors

6   Hot glue gun and glue sticks

7   Tacky craft glue

8   Craft wire

9   Ribbon or twine

10 Fine craft tweezers

11 Small stapler

12 Pencil

13 Paper brads

14 Stiletto

15 Embossing tool

16 Ruler

THE PROJECTS

SIMPLE PAPER POM-POM

Pom-poms made with tissue paper are a fun and very pretty way to decorate your home. This basic pom-pom is extremely easy and quick to make and yet provides a magical display for a special occasion. One of the best things about this project is that you can make the poms in any size and color, so feel free to experiment. In no time at all you can create multiple pom-poms in various sizes and different color combinations. Try hanging these beautiful puffs in clusters, close to the ceiling or low over a table setting, where they will make a dense and eyecatching "cloud" overhead. Be sure to hang some of the pom-poms lower than others to give some serious pizazz to your room.

how to make it

Once you master this, you will have the basic skills for all of the projects in this book. All sizes here are given as a guide, so you can make your pom-pom as large or small as you wish. The width of the paper gives the approximate diameter of the finished pom-pom, and the number of layers of tissue paper determine the amount of ruffles.

you will need

8 sheets of 10 x 14½ in. (25.5 x 37cm) tissue paper in colors of your choice

26-gauge (0.4 mm) craft wire

Strong scissors

Ruler

Bone folder (optional)

Tip

The excess length of wire in Step 4 can be used to wrap around ribbon to hang the pom-pom. If you're creating a larger pom-pom, use a thicker, stronger wire.

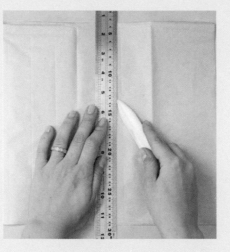

1 Stack all the sheets of tissue paper together. Make scoring marks at intervals of 1½ in. (4 cm) along the length of the paper.

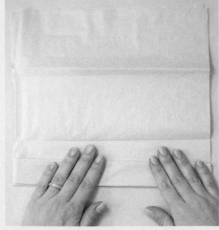

2 Fold the paper along the scored lines in accordion folds, creasing with each fold.

3 Fold the stack of pleated tissue paper in half to find the center.

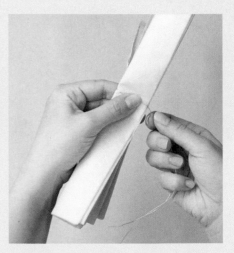

4 Cut a piece of wire about 2 in. (5 cm) longer than the width of the paper. Fold the wire in half, place around the center of the folded tissue and twist both ends to secure.

variation *Use more layers in a wider and longer length for a bigger, puffier pom-pom. Cut the ends into an inverted "V" shape rather than a rounded edge in Step 5 for a sharper, pointy look to your pom-pom.*

5 With scissors, trim both ends of the tissue stack to give them a rounded shape.

6 Carefully separate the layers of tissue, pulling away from the center one at a time until you have a puffy, rounded pom-pom.

GIFT BOX TOPPER

Wrapping gifts is an activity that I have always enjoyed, but purchasing lots of lavish ribbons, bows, and tags to create stand-out pieces can prove to be expensive. Making a fluffy pom-pom to adorn a simple gift box immediately adds the "wow" factor. Do-it-yourself details can make a big impact and will always be appreciated by your friends and family. Alter the size or color of your pom-pom topper to match your gift box, or wrap your present in three sheets of tissue paper in a complementary color before adding the pom-pom as a finishing touch.

variation (below left) *Change the look with a two-color variation. Choose two shades of a plain color in tissue paper and stack one on top of the other in Step 1 (page 17). Or alternate the colors when stacking for a more integrated color change.*

how to make it

The technique used in this project is similar to the Simple Paper Pom-Pom (see pages 10–13), but rather than creating a fully rounded shape, these pom-poms are semi-circular with a flat bottom for attaching to the top of your gift boxes and gift-wrapped presents.

you will need

6 sheets of 7½ x 10 in. (19 x 25.5 cm)
   tissue paper in colors of your choice
26-gauge (0.4 mm) craft wire
Strong scissors
Ruler
Craft glue

Tip

I wrapped my present in three layers of tissue paper but you can use other papers, including brown or sugar paper. It's the large pom-pom on the top that grabs the attention.

1 Stack the tissue paper together. Make scoring marks at intervals of 1 in. (2.5 cm). Make accordion folds along the scored lines, making sure to crease each fold well.

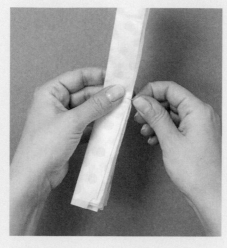

2 Fold the pleated stack in half to find the center. Wrap a short piece of wire around the middle and twist both ends together to secure.

3 Trim one end of the tissue paper stack into an inverted "V" or pointed shape.

4 Fold the tissue in half, then use the trimmed end as a guide to cut the other end so that they are the same height and shape.

5 Carefully ruffle the layers upwards rather than half up, half down as you did for the Simple Pom-Pom until you have a puffy semi-circle.

6 Add a small dab of glue to the back of the pom-pom and attach to a wrapped gift.

ICE-CREAM CONE

Children's parties and ice cream go hand-in-hand, so what better decoration could you choose than pom-pom balls of ice cream in waffle cones? All you need to do is decide on your color scheme, get the kids involved and you'll make a colorful statement with this lively project. Here, the colors of the pom-poms call to mind the delicious flavours of vanilla, strawberry, chocolate, and pistachio, but bold, playful, primary colored pom-poms would also work to brighten up the table and add to the party atmosphere. If you make plenty of them, you can let each child take one away as a party gift — you'll be remembered as the perfect host.

variation (right) *Following the ice cream theme, use a cup rather than a cone. Hide a small trinket or gift inside the cup for your party guests. Use a smaller sized pom-pom for the cup, made from eight sheets of tissue paper measuring 9 x 11 in. (23 x 28 cm), so that the finished size is approximately 8 in. (20 cm) in diameter.*

how to make it

You can make these ice-cream cones in any size by adjusting the diameter of the circle for the cone and the length of tissue paper. Make the cone first, measure the open-top diameter and create a pom-pom to fit.

you will need

Tissue paper in colors of your choice

26-gauge (0.4 mm) craft wire

Thick brown paper

Brown ink pad and sponge

Bone folder and ruler

Hot glue gun

1 Cut out a circle with a 10 in. (25.5 cm) diameter from thick brown paper. You can use a large plate as template for this.

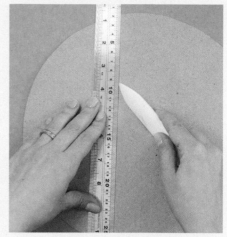

2 Make parallel scoring lines across the circle. Turn the circle by 30° and repeat the scoring to create a diamond pattern. Using a sponge, dab brown ink over the pattern to add more definition.

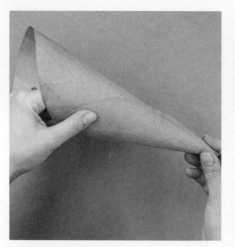

3 Using a hot glue gun, add glue along the inside edge of the circle and roll into a cone shape. Hold the cone until the glue bonds well, then set aside.

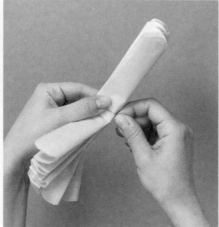

4 Make a pom-pom using the steps of Simple Paper Pom-Pom (see pages 10–13) but with tissue paper of 12 x 10 in. (30.5 x 25.5 cm) and fold it at ½ in. (1 cm) intervals.

5 Pipe glue around the top edge of the cone and attach the pom-pom on top.

FAIRY LIGHTS

This delicate project shows how to add pom-pom frills to a set of fairy or string lights for a simple yet sophisticated decoration. It's an effective way to add a special touch to a set of ordinary white lights and you'll find that they're perfect for so many occasions. Here, I've used a simple white tissue paper with a golden fleck that catches the light, making them ideal to hang as a garland at a birthday celebration or a wedding reception. However, this project can easily be adapted by using different types and weights of paper and colors – choose from glitter and metallic to patterned or striped designs depending on the occasion.

how to make it

The pom-pom frills in this project can be quite time-consuming, simply because you'll need to make up a large number for a single set of lights. To speed things up, work out how many tissue paper circles you'll need at the outset and cut out together in batches.

you will need

3 tissue paper circles per light, with a
diameter of 3 in. (7.5 cm) in a color
of your choice
Scissors
Craft glue
Tissue or masking tape
(washi tape is good for this)
Set of fairy or string lights

1 Cut out three tissue paper circles and layer them together.

2 Fold and scrunch them together in the center to create a point.

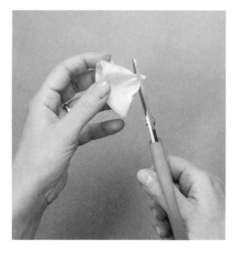

3 Using scissors, cut off the very end of the center point.

4 Separate the three layers. Add a ring of glue around the edge of the hole of each circle and stick all three layers together.

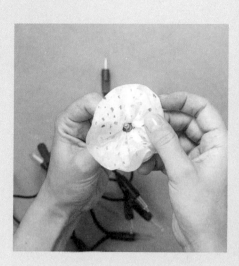

5 Gently place the tissue paper stack over the top of one bulb of the lights.

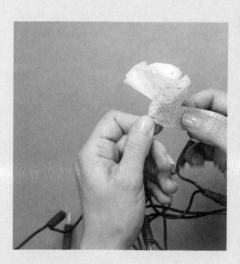

6 Secure at the base using tissue or masking tape. Ruffle the edges of the paper into a frill. Repeat to cover all the lights.

HOUSE PLANT

I love having plants in my home but they can be difficult to care for. This clever project is the ideal solution – making these miniature trees from tissue paper allows me to keep greenery around the home that doesn't require any care at all! The project is very versatile, as you don't just have to make pom-pom trees – you can make these everlasting plants in different sizes and colors. Try using tissue paper in deep pink or purple to create pom-poms that represent oversized dahlias. You can also alter the appearance with different lengths of twig or branch or by choosing a more heavily embellished plant pot.

how to make it

You can adapt the size of the pom-pom to suit any plant pot that you have at home. Here, I've created a tree of around 13 in. (33 cm) in height and 6¾ in. (17 cm) in diameter, which is ideal for a table or window-ledge decoration.

you will need

Tissue paper in several shades of green

Wire

Hot glue gun

Twig or branch

Strong scissors

Floral foam

Plant pot

variation (far right) Make a tall version of the tree. You'll need approximately 14 layers of tissue paper measuring 14 x 20 in. (35.5 x 51 cm). Make the folds around 2 in. (5 cm) apart and the fringe cuts to around 2 in. (5 cm) deep. You'll need a plant pot that is approximately 5 in. (13 cm) wide at the top.

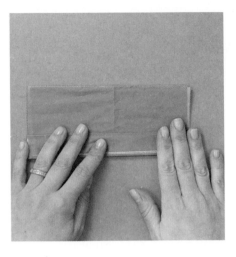

1 Cut eight pieces of tissue paper (2 or 3 of each shade) measuring 6½ x 9 in. (16.5 x 23 cm). Layer together, alternating one of each shade and fold in ¾ in. (2 cm) accordion folds.

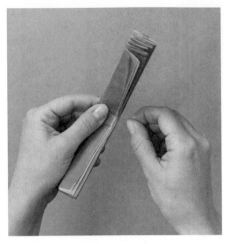

2 Tie the pleated stack in the center with wire and twist tightly to secure.

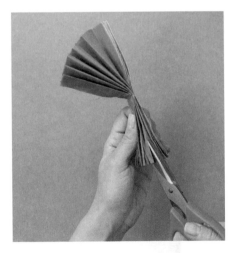

3 Using strong scissors, cut into the folds about 1 in. (2.5 cm) deep from the outer edge on both sides of the pom-pom.

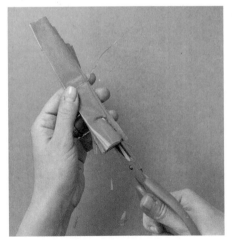

4 Make 1 in. (2.5 cm) deep, thin parallel cuts to create a fringe. Cut through several layers at a time but not all, as the scissors will struggle.

5 Very gently separate the layers — pulling from the center rather than from the fringed edges. Puff the edges out until you have a semi-circle.

6 Using a hot glue gun, attach a dry twig to the center of the pom-pom at the back.

7 Repeat Steps 1–5 to create the other half of the plant and, using hot glue, attach to the first half to create a full pom-pom.

8 Secure a piece of floral foam inside your plant pot and insert the bottom of the twig. You can hide the floral foam and create more stability to the pot by adding sand.

BRIDAL BOUQUET

As a bride, you may not wish to use natural flowers on your wedding day – real flowers can look very beautiful but quickly fade, whereas pom-pom flowers will last forever! This pom-pom bouquet is the perfect alternative. Making your own bouquet also adds an individual touch to the occasion. The cost of materials is fairly minimal in comparison to a natural flower bouquet and the time it takes to make can be enjoyed in the company of your bridesmaids, who can make up their own bouquets in a complementary color. This sumptuous bouquet is made from coffee filters, using a color palette of deep reds, oranges and yellows, but a more traditional look of whites, creams or pastel shades would be just as stunning, as illustrated in the decoration pictured on the right.

variation (right) *This project works really well without colored inks – off-white paper is perfect for wedding decorations. As with the bouquet, you can pin the coffee filters all around the polystyrene ball, or, as shown here, just add to the top half and then place in a cupcake/muffin liner. Rather than attaching the flowers with faux crystal pins, I've used pearls for a softer look.*

how to make it

Choose the accents and embellishments for your bouquet before you start — think about the look of the ribbon that you'd like to wrap around the bouquet handle and the type of pins you want to use for the center of the flower heads. Here, I've used faux crystal pins but you can choose any decorative pins. Any coffee filters will work, but I've used Size 4, which measure 7½ x 5 in. (19 x 12.5 cm) when folded flat.

you will need

Polystyrene ball (4¾ in. (12 cm)
    in diameter)
Bouquet handle
White ribbon
Coffee filters
Faux crystal pins
Color sprays in red, orange, amber,
    and yellow
Polystyrene block (or some leftover
    packaging)
Green cardstock
Hot glue gun
Recommended: die-cutting machine
    and circle die

1 Attach the polystyrene ball to the bouquet handle. You may need to secure it with hot glue around the base.

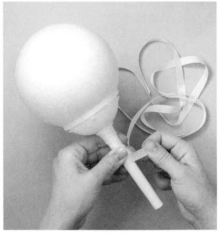

2 Wind a long length of ribbon around the handle, starting at the top and working down to the bottom. Secure the ribbon at both ends with a dab of hot glue.

3 Using coffee filters, cut out approximately 240 circles with a diameter of 2 in. (5 cm) and arrange into stacks of six circles. This creates 40 flowers, which should cover your bouquet, depending on how tightly they are packed together. A die-cutting machine will make this process much quicker and more precise.

Tip

Use permanent color sprays to avoid the flowers becoming stained, if they get wet. For a more realistic look to the leaves, you can stamp them with green ink (see Brooch/Boutonnière project, page 37).

4 Pin each set of six layers through the center onto a polystyrene block (or leftover piece of packaging). Pack them together tightly and ruffle the sides of the filters into flower shapes.

5 Cover your work surface with protective paper before spraying the flowers with different colors. Start with a generous layer of the lighter colors and use darker colors more sparingly.

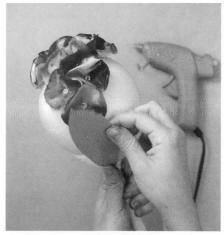

6 Make sure that you spray the sides of the flowers, although inevitably some layers won't get any ink. Leave to dry completely.

7 Start placing the flowers onto the polystyrene ball with the faux crystal pins. Pack together tightly so that the polystyrene ball is completely concealed.

8 Using the templates on page 90, cut approximately 15 leaves in different sizes from the green card. Using hot glue, attach the leaves to the bottom of polystyrene ball.

BROOCH | BOUTONNIÈRE

Make a statement with this radiant boutonnière or brooch. You can adapt the style of this project to suit the occasion. Here, I've made one in bright yellow for a little girl's outfit, but you can use several shades or add extra layers of tissue paper for a fuller, more traditional look. As with the Crepe Paper Flowers on pages 50-53, attach a pipe cleaner as a little stem at the back to create the boutonnière. This paper floral brooch has advantages over a natural flower – you can make it well in advance, it can be worn more than once, and can be kept as a keepsake after a special event.

variation (bottom left) Change the colors of each size circle in Step 1 (page 36) to create a different flower. Or use a larger, glittery paper brad for the center of your brooch – it will appeal to little girls even more! You can ruffle the layers of the flower as much or as little as you want, but remember to be gentle as the tissue paper can tear easily.

how to make it

In this project, I've used a number of specialized paper tools, such as a piercing tool and an embossing tool. These are optional and you will still be able to complete the project without them, but they do help to create a professional finish to your brooch.

you will need

Tissue paper in yellow or color of your choice

Green cardstock

Paper brad

Mouse pad or embossing mat

Green ink pad

Strong scissors

Brooch clasp

Paper piercing tool (optional)

Paper embossing tool (optional)

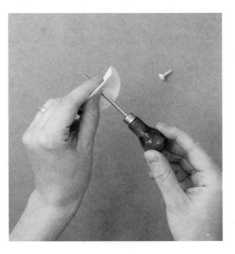

1 Cut six circles from each of the following diameters: 2, 1¾ and 1½ in. (5, 4.5 and 4 cm). Starting with the largest size, layer these together and pierce them in the center with a paper piercing tool.

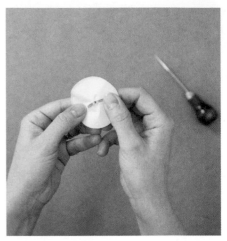

2 Place a paper brad through the hole in the center and secure it at the back by opening the legs.

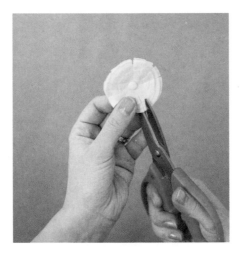

3 Starting from the outer edge, make straight radial cuts to approximately ¼ in. (6 mm) from the paper brad all the way around the circumference, at even intervals.

4 Very gently scrunch the tissue paper to make petals, lifting each layer towards the center until you have a rounded shape.

5 Using the templates on page 95, trace around two different sized leaf shapes onto green cardstock.

6 Place the larger leaf on the back of a mouse pad or similar soft foam mat. Using a paper embossing tool, draw the veins of the leaf freehand.

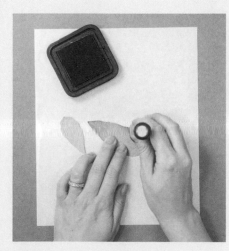

7 Using a piece of foam, dab green ink over the leaf to accentuate the veins. Repeat Steps 6–7 for the smaller leaf.

8 Layer the smaller leaf on top of the larger one, and attach to the pom-pom flower with hot glue. Finally, secure the brooch clasp onto the back of the large leaf.

Tip

For the correct sizing to match the flower, it's best to photocopy the leaf templates at 100%. Using a foam tool applicator for applying the ink will create a better result.

DOILY DECORATION

The old-fashioned and timeless appeal of doilies means that they are the ideal material for this charming paper-craft project. You can use these hanging doily pom-poms as decorations for weddings, christening parties, baby showers or even to give a child's bedroom that delicate vintage vibe. Appearing to float in the air, these prisitine white doilies give a classic feel but you could try a brighter theme using different colored paper doilies for a more vibrant effect. These hanging ornaments are also particularly effective when used in multiples of different sizes.

how to make it

Paper doilies are available in different sizes, colors, and patterns, and are ideal for textured and intricate-looking pom-poms. Scrunching the doilies to create the ruffle effect is quite time-consuming, but once you've completed a set the construction of the pom-pom is straightforward.

you will need

Doilies (any size will work, these are 4½ in. (11 cm) in diameter)

Hot glue gun

Heat mat or embossing mat

Baker's twine

Scissors

Tip

You will need about 20 doilies for a very full, hanging pom-pom but you can use fewer for a simpler one.

1 Fold one doily in half and open again.

2 Fold the doily once more to create four quarters. Then open again.

3 Repeat the folds in Steps 1 and 2 but this time fold it at 45° from the other folds so that you create eight sections.

4 Following the fold lines push four opposite sections towards the center, so that when folded it looks like a quarter of a circle.

5 Repeat Steps 1–4 with five more identical doilies so that you have a set of six.

6 Place a dab of hot glue onto a heat resistant surface and attach four folded doilies to create a full circle.

7 Add a little more hot glue on the top of the circle in the center and attach a fifth folded doily.

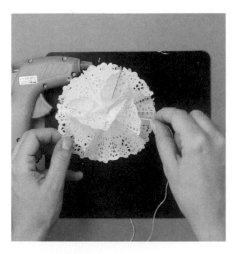

8 When the glue has set, turn over the doilies and glue the sixth folded doily in the center. Attach a length of baker's twine or your choice of ribbon in the center with hot glue.

variation (left) *To make a simpler doily decoration, fold five (or more) doilies in half. Then glue the back of the left side of one doily to the back of the right side of the next one , and so on. Attach baker's twine on the spine of the doilies. This works well on these heart-shaped doilies.*

FLOWER TABLE DECORATION

Make a bold statement with these oversized, beautiful pom-pom flowers, which will add a cheerful radiance to a dinner party or rehearsal dinner. Using a creative method of layering the tissue paper, the vivid colors in the pom-pom petals combine to create an eye-catching centerpiece for a table setting. Alternatively, these can be hung from the branches of trees in the garden or the rafters of gazebos and porches, or attached to stems and arranged in a vase (see also pages 50-53). Try doubling them up for a super-sized flower.

variation (above) Make a compact version and attach a pin holder for a place setting. Use nine sheets of tissue paper, all measuring 4 x 8 in. (10 x 20 cm) and fold in one go. Instead of fringing the green paper, trim it short after ruffling out the layers of tissue paper at the end. For the smaller version in the color palette shown opposite, use two sheets in green, five in light pink and two in dark pink.

how to make it

The bright, bold colors demonstrated here will always brighten someone's day. You can change the colors and the sizes — you just need to ensure that the pieces of tissue paper are in proportion to each other.

you will need

Tissue paper in assorted colors (dark pink, light pink, dark green, and light green)

26-gauge (0.4 mm) craft wire

Strong scissors

Pencil

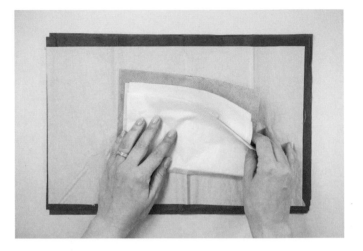

1 Cut two pieces of dark pink tissue paper to measure 14½ x 9½ in. (37 x 24 cm), six pieces of light pink to measure 13½ x 8½ in. (34 x 21 cm), one dark green at 8 x 5 in. (20 x 13 cm) and three light green at 7½ x 4½ in. (19 x 11 cm).

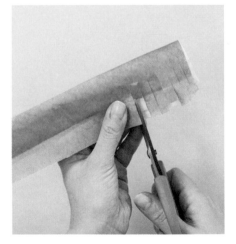

2 Layer the light green paper on top of the dark green and fold in half lengthwise. Make parallel cuts up to 1 in. (2.5 cm) from the folded edge and open out.

3 Center on top of the pink, with the light pink on top of the dark. Make a light pencil mark at the point where the green papers start.

4 Remove the green paper and start folding the pinks in 1 in. (2.5 cm) accordion folds.

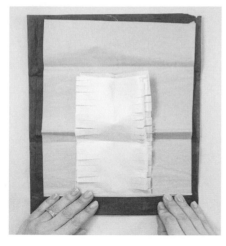

5 When you reach the pencil mark, place the green papers back on top and continue to fold to the end.

6 Separate the layers by color and cut the ends of both pink papers into a pronounced arch.

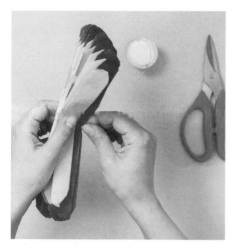

7 Layer all the papers together once again, making sure that the folds are aligned and fold them back into their pleated shape.

8 Attach a piece of wire at the center and twist the ends to secure.

9 Fan the pleats out into the center and gently open one layer at a time, ruffling the tissue paper.

Tip

Take extra care when ruffling the green elements as they are very delicate and some pieces may break off.

TASSEL GARLAND

With their origins and inspiration in the style of a traditional cheerleader's pom-pom, paper tassels are a variety of pom-pom that can be used to make a charming and versatile display. This gorgeous garland looks wonderful when strung around the room at a wedding venue, such as a marquee, a barn, or in the garden. You could also use this garland as alternative bunting at a birthday party or to add a splash of color to a nursery wall. With only a few tools required, you can alter the basic technique to create different effects.

how to make it

The garland that I've made here is approximately 7 ft (2 m) in length and includes six of the main tassels, along with five tassels in a longer length. Make the longer tassel by starting with four layers of tissue paper cut to measure 4½ x 25 in. (11 x 64 cm). You use more or fewer tassels to create a different visual effect.

you will need

Tissue paper in colors of your choice

26-gauge (0.4 mm) craft wire

Strong scissors

Ruler

Cutting mat

Rotary cutter

Paper clips

Paper brad

Ribbon

Quilting ruler (optional)

1 Cut three sheets of tissue paper to 15 x 9½ in. (38 x 24 cm) and layer together. Find the vertical center line of the longest edge and, with a pencil, mark a point at 2 in. (5 cm) from the center.

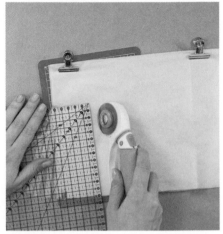

2 Fold the paper stack in half along the vertical center line with the pencil mark on the outside. Secure with paper clips along the fold. Place on a cutting mat and, with the rotary cutter, make a cut up from the bottom edge to the pencil mark.

3 Continue cutting in this way to create thin strips all the way along the paper.

4 Unclip and unfold from the center and start rolling the papers together from one edge to the other.

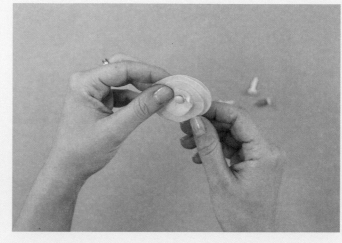

5 Fold the rolled paper in half and set aside for now.

6 Using the templates on page 91, cut three circles with diameters of 2, 1½ and 1 in. (5, 4 and 2.5 cm). Stack these in size order with the largest at the bottom and place a paper brad through the middle. (Alternatively, glue the layers together and use a sticker for the center.)

7 Thread a long piece of ribbon through the middle of the pom-pom tassel and secure in place with wire.

8 Glue the paper circles to the top of the tassel, covering the wire. Repeat Steps 1–6 to make further tassels and attach at intervals along the ribbon to create a garland.

CREPE PAPER FLOWERS

Making paper flowers is one of my passions – the finished result is very satisfying and you can make them in so many different ways. This project shows just one way of making a delicate, appealing bloom using crepe paper. My inspiration here was a romantic Heirloom Peony, notable for its full blossom and wonderful fragrance. The beauty of this project is that each flower will always be slightly different from the next one you make, just like real flowers. Make a handful of these stemmed flowers, find a selection of elegant glass bottles and you can create a gorgeous display for a dressing table or mantel piece.

variation (right) *Change the number of petals to create different flowers. Use only the larger petals to create a rose shape as shown in some of the yellow flowers. Roll the inner petal around the wire and continue rolling petals around. For smaller flowers, reduce the size of the petals to around 80% when photocopying the templates.*

how to make it

When you cut out the petal shapes in Step 3, make sure that the lines of the crepe paper run vertically – this will allow you to shape and curl the petals by pulling or stretching them sideways. The largest of my flowers is about 4 in. (10 cm) in diameter (across the flower head) and 3 in. (8 cm) tall (from the base to the top of the petals). The smaller ones are about 2 in. (5 cm) in diameter and about 2 in. (5cm) tall.

you will need

Thick crepe paper (180 gsm) in soft pink, white, yellow, and pale green

Florist wire

Florist waxed tape

PVA glue

Pipe cleaners – 12 in. (30.5 cm) in length

Strong scissors

Small polystyrene ball – approximately ½ in. (1 cm) in diameter

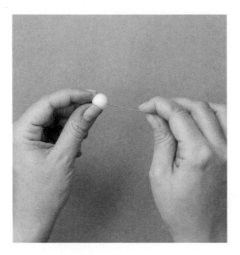

1 Insert the end of a 4-in. (10-cm) length of florist wire into the polystyrene ball. Use a small amount of glue to secure it in place.

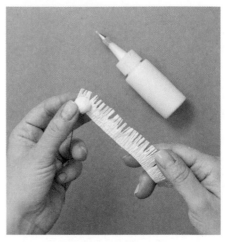

2 Cut a piece of yellow crepe paper to 6 in. (15 cm) in length and ¾ in. (2 cm) tall. Make very thin, parallel cuts along the length. Then, add a thin line of glue along the length and roll it around the ball.

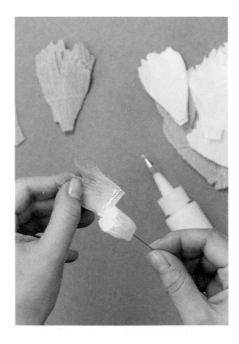

3 Using the templates on page 92, cut three to four of each petal (four for the largest petal) in pink crepe paper. Then cut four each of the two largest petals in white crepe paper. Starting with the smaller pink petals, add some glue at the bottom and attach evenly around the center ball.

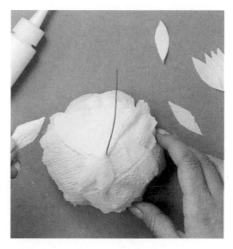

4 Continue attaching the pink petals, increasing in size and spreading them evenly around to create a flower shape. If necessary, trim the ends of some petals to make them shorter.

5 Once you have added all of the smaller pink petals, add the large white petals, alternating with a couple of large pink ones to create a subtle ombre effect.

6 Cut four large petals in green crepe paper. Trim the bottoms by ½ in. (1 cm), so that they don't show over the top of the white petals and attach around the base of the flower. Then cut around eight small leaves and attach in a circle at the base.

7 Wrap the wire end around five pipe cleaners to create a stem. You can use fewer pipe cleaners for a thinner stem.

8 Starting at the base of the flower head, wrap florist wax tape down around the pipe cleaners, pulling gently to activate the wax.

Tip

When cutting the petals don't worry about being too precise – the more rugged you make the top part, the better.

BUTTERFLY

When summer is in full bloom, butterflies are welcome visitors to the garden. Celebrate the magic of these delicate creatures with this pom-pom project – a lovely, decorative idea that will brighten up a plain wall. These delightful butterflies can make a girl's bedroom come alive in a joyous burst of color! Or create an unusual backdrop on a garden wall for a summer party or Fourth of July barbecue. Why not connect a string of butterflies in varying colors and sizes to create a dazzling garland and hang in front of an open window so that they flutter in the breeze.

how to make it

While this project may look complicated at first glance, it is actually a clever adaptation of the technique used in the Simple Paper Pom-Pom (see pages 10–13). Take care when layering the tissue paper and you will end up with a neat finished look.

you will need

Tissue paper in two matching colors –
   one light and one dark
Scissors
26-gauge (0.4 mm) craft wire
Thick black wire
Hot glue gun
Black glitter

1 Cut four sheets of lighter colored tissue paper to measure 14 x 9½ in. (35.5 x 24 cm) and another four sheets to 7 x 14 in. (18 x 35.5 cm). Then, cut two sheets of the darker paper to measure 7 x 10 in. (18 x 25.5 cm) and another two sheets to 5 x 7½ in. (13 x 19 cm).

2 Layer the larger pieces of each color together and then the smaller pieces on top. Fold the layers in accordion folds at intervals of 1 in. (2.5 cm) and then separate the different sized stacks.

3 Fold the larger of the dark colored pleated stacks in half and cut the ends to create a rounded shape.

4 Layer this back over the larger pleated stack of the light colored paper. Fold in half and trim the ends of the light paper into a rounded shape.

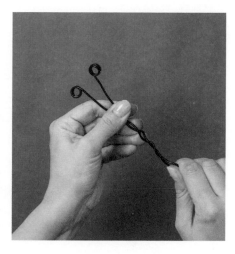

5 Repeat Steps 3 and 4 with the set of smaller papers in the two colors. Join both pleated stacks together at the center with a piece of wire and twist to secure.

6 To make the butterfly antennae and body, cut a piece of black wire to the same length as the wingspan and fold it in half. Then coil each end around a pencil.

7 Twist the wire up to the halfway point to create the butterfly body, leaving the two antennae separate.

8 Fan open the wings. Apply a few lines of hot glue across the back to hold them open. Once dry, glue the wire body to the front of the wings. Add a sprinkle of black glitter to disguise the join and add sparkle!

variation (above) *Try a simpler version of the butterfly by making only one section for the wings – either the large or the small ones. You can also use the template on page 92 to cut out a body from cardstock instead of using wire.*

HONEYCOMB
POM-POM

Honeycomb-effect paper pom-poms are a great way to create small or large home and party decor. With little more than glue, ribbon and paper, you can transform a space. Even the most cramped reception room can feel light and airy with the addition of these spectacular looking pom-poms. Not only can honeycomb pom-poms be hung from the ceiling in elegant clusters or made into colorful garlands, they can also be arranged on the floor or sit on a shelf as an interesting art display.

variation (bottom right) *This honeycomb pom-pom is very versatile and you can have so much fun with it. For this variation cut the layered semi-circle into a triangle shape, keeping the base of the semi-circle as the base of the triangle. Attach a piece of cord from the base of the triangle up through the point and then fan the honeycomb open vertically for this different effect.*

how to make it

You can buy honeycomb paper readymade, which is then simple to cut into a semi-circle and turn into a three-dimensional shape, but if you want to try out your craft skills and create a perfectly matched rainbow honeycomb, you should make your own. This is how you do it.

you will need

24 tissue paper circles with a diameter of
   7½ in. (19 cm) in colors of your choice

Strong scissors

Tacky glue

Fine-nozzle glue dispenser

2 pieces of colored cardstock to match
   the tissue paper

Ribbon

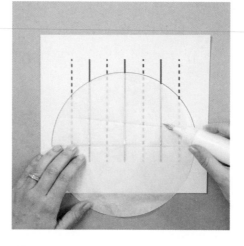

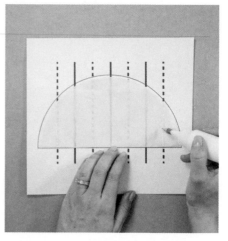

1 Photocopy the template on page 93 at 100%. Fold a tissue paper circle in half, then open it up and position on the template semi-circle. Using the solid lines as a guide, apply three thin lines of glue. Fold the circle in half and press until the glue sets.

2 Place the semi-circle back on the template. Add four fine lines of glue following the dashed lines and then add a further fine line along the straight edge of the bottom fold. The less glue you use the better.

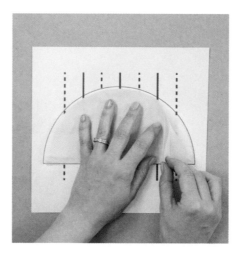

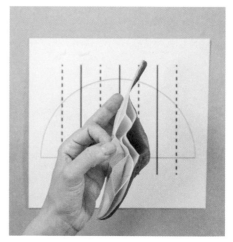

3 Repeat Step 1 with a different colored tissue paper circle and place it over the first semi-circle.

4 Repeat Steps 1–3, using alternating colors of tissue paper, until you have glued all 24 circles in place. You will see that the honeycomb effect starts to take place.

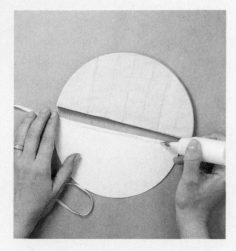

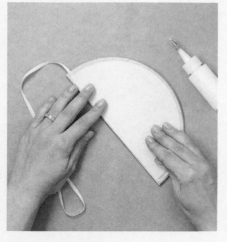

5 Using a similar colored card to the top layer of tissue paper, cut a semi-circle of the same size. Glue a piece of ribbon along the straight edge of the cardstock.

6 Glue the cardstock onto the tissue paper semi-circle with the ribbon on the inside.

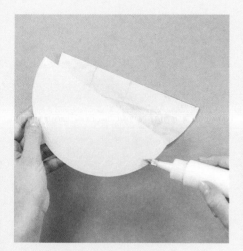

7 Cut another semi-circle piece of cardstock – this time to match the color of the other end of the tissue paper honeycomb. Glue onto the honeycomb. Leave to set.

8 Open out the pom-pom and secure the two sides of cardstock together with glue or small paper clips (clips are a good idea, if you want to fold back safely and store flat).

SNOWMAN

Creating a pom-pom snowman is a fun activity for the whole family for the Winter season and it can be used to add some festive sparkle to your home. This charming snowman makes a friendly addition to a window sill or mantelpiece. With lots of cute options for traditional snowman embellishments such as hats, noses, buttons, and scarves, kids will be inspired to make their own little family of snowmen and women. So spread some Christmas cheer with this delightful frosty fellow – made from paper, he'll never melt!

how to make it

This pom-pom snowman has been made to a height of approximately 22 in. (56 cm) but you can make it in any size that you want, as long as you increase (or decrease) the size of the individual pom-poms for the head and body proportionally.

you will need

White tissue paper

Hot glue gun

26-gauge (0.4 mm) craft wire

Orange paper

Black buttons

Wooden rod (at least 20 in./51 cm long)

Ribbon (optional)

Tip

If the cone seems a little big when making the snowman's nose, trim a small amount from the open end before gluing in place.

1 To make the head: cut six sheets of white tissue paper to 5 x 9 in. (13 x 23 cm). Layer together and fold in 1-in. (2.5-cm) accordion folds. Repeat this process with another six sheets.

2 Bind the folded stacks together at the center with a piece of wire. Gently separate and ruffle the layers of tissue until you have two rounded pom-poms.

3 Using a hot glue gun, attach one of the pom-poms to the wooden rod. If you're adding a hat, leave 3 in. (7.5 cm) at the top of the rod for this. Once secure, add the second pom-pom at the back of the first.

4 For the middle section of the body: repeat Steps 1–2, but starting with eight sheets of tissue paper cut to 7 x 12 in. (18 x 30.5 cm). Attach these two pom-poms to the rod below the head, as in Step 3.

variation (below) *Make a smaller version of the snowman with only two pom-pom parts instead of three. Finish the look by gluing a ribbon around his neck for a scarf and make a simple hat from a rolled piece of cardstock.*

5 Cut a 5-in. (13-cm) circle from orange paper, roll it into a cone and glue together. Fix this in the center of the top pom-pom as a nose.

6 Using a dab of glue, add two black buttons above the nose for eyes. Add the bottom section of the body by repeating Steps 1–3, starting with eight sheets cut to 9 x 15 in. (23 x 38 cm).

HEART KEEPSAKE

If you're a book lover, you may find it hard to come to terms with cutting out pages from a book at first, but this beautiful project is a wonderful way to recycle a battered old book and add some vintage style to your home. This charming heart would make the perfect Valentine's Day gift or decoration to adorn a wedding venue. You could even adapt the project to make multiple smaller hearts as wedding favors. Using recycled pages means that making this delicate heart can also be a good way to practice your crafting skills without having to spend much money.

variation (left) *Why not try this idea using a heart-shaped chocolate box lid? Cover the box lid with strips of paper as shown in Steps 1–2 (page 68). Then, create the spirals and glue in a heart shape inside the lid. This technique lends itself to so many options and shapes, including the small wreath pictured top left.*

how to make it

This is a great project to make over multiple crafting sessions – cutting, rolling, and gluing the spirals can be done in separate stages. Remember that old book pages can be brittle and the acid and lignin in the paper can make it yellow with time but this is part of the charm of the vintage look.

you will need

Pages from an old book

A polystyrene heart, approximately
    8 in. (20 cm)

Chunky glitter in champagne color

Quilling tool

Matte decoupage medium

Hot glue gun

PVA glue

Paintbrush

Pencil

Scissors

1 Tear the pages of your book into strips of different sizes. Using a clean, dry brush, apply matte decoupage medium over a small area of the polystyrene heart.

2 Place a strip of paper on top and cover it with matte decoupage medium. Repeat this process until the whole heart is covered in paper.

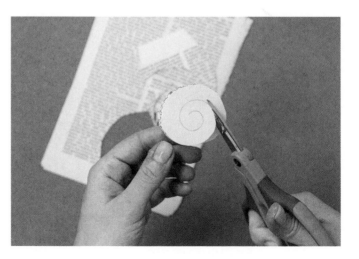

3 Using the template on page 93, cut out a 2-in. (5-cm) circle from a page of the book (it doesn't need to be precise.) Draw and cut the inward spiral in the circle.

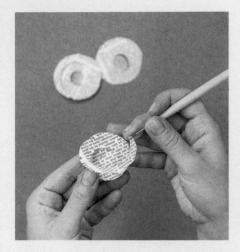 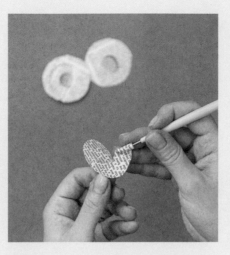 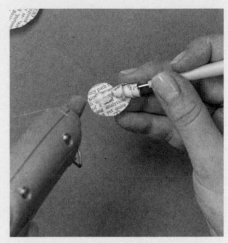

4 Using a quilling tool – the end looks like an open sewing needle – start rolling the outer end of the spiral into the center.

5 Continue rolling inwards, keeping the rolled-up paper tight until you've nearly reached the center.

6 Apply hot glue in the center of the spiral. Remove the quilling tool from the paper and push the rolled up paper onto the glue in the center.

 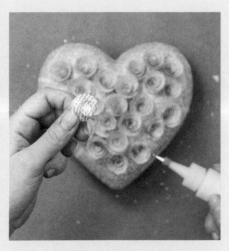

7 While the glue is setting, sprinkle some chunky glitter over it. Once the glue cools, shake off any excess glitter and put it back in the pot ready for the next spiral.

8 Once you have made enough spirals, attach them to the surface of the heart with a dab of PVA glue or hot glue on the back.

Tip

To speed up the process of making this heart, I layer three book pages together in Step 3 and cut out three spirals at a time.

EASTER BANNER

Make this cheerful banner to decorate your home – it's perfect for an Easter celebration. The pastel shades and embellishments used on the bunting evoke a wonderful sense of spring and rebirth. You can also adapt the colors to suit other occasions – a birthday celebration, a baby shower, or a summer party. Change the egg pom-pom to a semi-circle pom-pom and add lettering to the bunting to create a personalized message.

how to make it

The banner I've created here is approximately 5 in. (13 cm) tall and has a total length of 10 ft. (3 m) but you can make one that is shorter or longer by using fewer or more rosettes and pom-poms, depending on the space you want to fill.

you will need

Tissue paper in purple, pink, blue, green and yellow

Cardstock in purple, pink, blue, green, white, and yellow

Wire

Hot glue gun

Scissors

Ribbon, approximately 10 ft. (3 m) in length

Double-sided tape

Embossing tool

Ruler

1 Using the templates on page 94, cut banner and bunting shapes from colored cardstock. Using the smaller banner template, cut pieces of white cardstock and attach onto the plain colored cardstock banners.

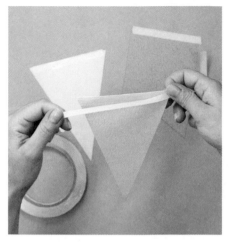

2 Attach these shapes to the ribbon at intervals, using double-sided tape. It is best to attach the tape to the cardstock first and then press the ribbon onto it.

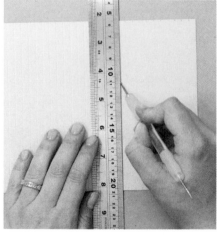

3 To make a rosette: cut a piece of cardstock to 8¾ x 6 in. (22 x 15 cm). This will make six rosettes. Make vertical parallel scoring lines across the length of the cardstock at ¼ in. (6 mm) intervals with an embossing tool.

4 Cut the cardstock into six horizontal strips of 1 in. (2.5 cm) in depth. Make accordion folds along the scored lines of each strip.

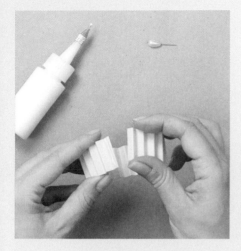

5 With a dab of glue, attach one end of the strip to the other so that it creates a complete ring.

6 Cut two circles from cardstock of 1 in. (2.5 cm) and ¾ in. (2 cm) in diameter. Put some hot glue on the larger circle and place the ring of cardstock on top. Gently push down towards the center with both hands until it flattens out, creating a rosette. Don't touch the center as hot glue may pour out. Hold until the glue has bonded, then glue the smaller circle on top in the center.

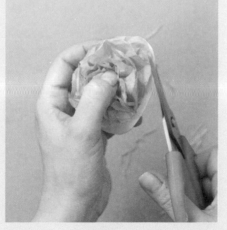

7 To make an egg pom-pom: cut eight layers of tissue paper to 4 x 5 in. (10 x 13 cm) and layer together. Fold the paper in ½ in. (1 cm) accordion folds. Tie the paper together with wire a ⅓ of the way in from one end.

8 Separate the layers to create a pom-pom. Using the egg template on page 94, trim the pom-pom into shape. You will need about 11 of these for this banner. Attach the rosettes and pom-poms to the banners and bunting.

Tip

Make a photocopy of all of the templates before you start, so that you can reuse them in the future.

PUMPKIN

Seasonal decorations for the home are a must and what is more appropriate for Halloween than a pumpkin? This tissue-paper pumpkin adds warmth and cheer to your home and can be used year after year, without the mess of carving a real pumpkin. Make multiples in varying sizes and group them together, but take care not to place them next to lighted candles! Original and effective, these pumpkins can be made with the help of your children, who can carry them trick-or-treating to impress the neighbours.

how to make it

Using a similar technique to the Simple Paper Pom-pom (see pages 10–13), the key to this project is keeping the bottom of the pom-pom flat. The addition of the stalk finishes off the effect. Here, the smaller pumpkin is made from tissue paper cut to 17 x 10 in. (17 x 25.5 cm) and the largest one from paper cut to 20 x 15 in. (51 x 38 cm).

you will need

8 sheets of 19 x 14 in. (48 x 35.5 cm)
   orange tissue paper

26-gauge (0.4 mm) craft wire

Strong scissors

Green cardstock

Green and brown ink pads

Hot glue gun

Bamboo stick

Foam tool applicator (optional)

1 Layer the eight sheets of tissue paper together and make accordion folds at intervals of 1½ in. (4 cm).

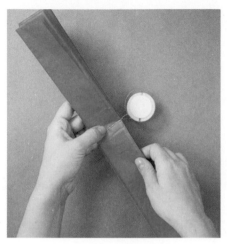

2 Fold the stack of paper in half to find the center and secure with a piece of wire.

3 Trim the edge of one end into a rounded shape, using strong scissors.

4 Use this rounded end as a guide to trim the other end.

Tip

The foam tool applicators are not essential for applying ink but they are really easy and practical. Alternatively, you can use a piece of kitchen sponge.

5 Carefully separate out the layers of tissue paper into a pom-pom shape, but keep the base flat. Glue a bamboo stick in the center of the pom-pom.

6 Using one of the templates on page 95, trace a stalk onto green cardstock and cut out. You will need two of these pieces.

7 Using the brown and green ink pads and foam tool applicators or a piece of foam, apply some color to the stalks.

8 Using hot glue, attach the stalk pieces to the bamboo stick in the center of the pom-pom, placing one on each side.

FESTIVE ORNAMENT

This gorgeous, frilly pom-pom ornament is cleverly made using cupcake liners or muffin cases, which most people have in their kitchen cupboard. This elegant sphere can be used as an accent on a mantelpiece or fire place and is a great decoration for an engagement party or wedding reception with its delicate, bridal feel. You can make these ornaments in other sizes, and by adding a strip of ribbon you can decorate your Christmas tree with little snowballs.

variation (right) *To make Christmas ornaments, use fairy cake liners, which are smaller than cupcake or muffin liners. For the core, use a smaller polystyrene ball and instead of inserting the twisted ends into the ball, trim them and use a hot glue gun to attach them to the ball (see Steps 4–5 on page 80).*

how to make it

The center of this project uses a polystyrene ball of approximately 2¾ in. (7 cm) in diameter. Choose a ball that matches the size of decoration you want to make.

you will need

Cupcake or muffin liners

Polystyrene ball of 2¾ in. (7cm) in diameter

Stiletto

Ribbon

Pin needle

Glue

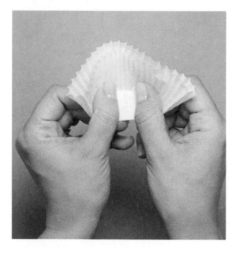

1 Fold one cupcake liner in half horizontally.

2 Fold the liner in half again, vertically this time, and then fold each end in opposite directions to create a zig-zag fold.

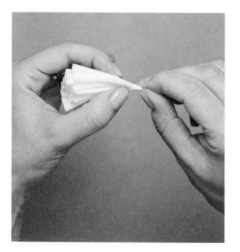

3 Twist the end tightly so that it creates a strong point.

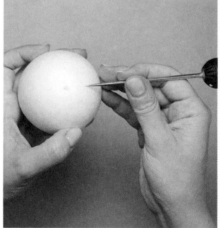

4 With a stiletto, poke a hole in the polystyrene ball. I like to use the "seam" that runs around the diameter to guide me at the beginning.

5 Press the point of the folded cupcake liner into the hole. Put a dab of glue in the hole to secure the liner in place.

6 Repeat steps 1–5 until there are a few liners on the ball. Then cut a length of ribbon that is roughly twice the height of the cupcake liners. Make a loop and pin the ribbon to the ball using a pin needle. Use a small amount of glue to secure the needle in place. Repeat Steps 1–5 until the whole ball is covered.

GIFT WRAPPING

Rustle up a picture-perfect present with this clever way to wrap perfumes, lotions and nail varnish bottles, and jars of jams and jellies. Creating an instant wow factor, this project also allows you to add a personal touch to gifts. Choose sheer sheets of tissue paper in a rainbow of colors, incorporating a delicate petal-like pom-pom at the end. Pick from the palest pinks and pastel colors for a charming selection of party favors or baby shower gifts, or ramp up the glamour by using a tissue paper with a striking pattern or a bold metallic finish, ideal for festive gifts and teenagers.

how to make it

This project has been demonstrated on a set of perfume bottles but you can adapt it to any cylindrical shape. Add more layers and colors for a taller item, such as a wine bottle. Decide on the color of Baker's twine to match your chosen tissue paper before you start.

you will need

Tissue paper in light pink and yellow

Cardstock in yellow

Clear sticky tape

Baker's twine

Scissors

1 Measure the height of your bottle – the yellow tissue paper needs to be about 2 in. (5 cm) taller than the bottle. Mark where the neck of the bottle starts.

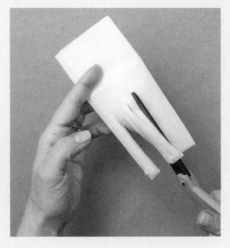

2 Cut the paper to 12 in. (30.5 cm) wide and as tall as required. Fold it several times, then cut thin strips from the top edge to the mark at the neck of the bottle.

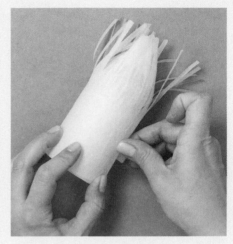

3 Unfold the paper, then roll it around the bottle. Secure the end of the paper with clear sticky tape.

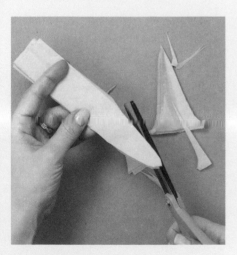

4 Cut two sheets of pink paper to approximately 3 in. (7.5 cm) taller than the bottle height and 24 in. (61 cm) wide. Layer together and fold in 1½ in. (4 cm) accordion folds. Trim one end into a long petal shape that reaches the height of the bottle neck.

5 Unfold the papers and roll them around the bottle one at a time. Secure the ends with sticky tape.

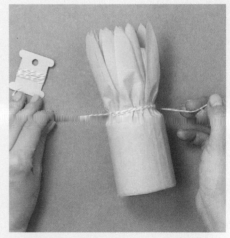

6 Tie the paper with baker's twine at the neck of the bottle and thread through a tag before making a knot, if desired.

CHRISTMAS WREATH

Welcome in the Christmas season by making this stunning tissue-paper wreath in rich festive colors evoking holly leaves, berries, and pine cones, which you can display proudly on the door to your home. There's nothing as satisfying as making your own seasonal decorations and this wreath creates an impressive display. Add to the elegant look of the wreath by attaching some matching colored ribbons as a tail for an exquisite finish. This gorgeous wreath is very versatile and would look special as a centerpiece for the table on Christmas Day or displayed as a statement piece over a mantelpiece. For a completely different look, choose silvers and golds that sparkle in the soft sunlight of a frosty winter's morning.

how to make it

It's useful to make this wreath in stages, creating all of the pom-pom flowers before mounting them on the cardboard to complete your wreath. You can create the pom-pom flowers in any size you wish, but the wreath looks more effective when you include a variety of sizes.

you will need

Tissue paper in light, medium and dark green, red and gold

Cardstock in green, red and gold

Cardboard

Hot glue gun

PVA glue

Scissors

Craft knife

Tip

If your front door is very exposed to the elements, try making this wreath with waterproof materials, such as colored film.

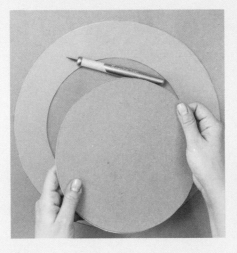

1 Use a large plate to draw a 12-in. (30.5-cm) diameter circle onto cardboard and cut out with scissors. Using a smaller plate of 8 in. (20 cm) diameter, draw an inner circle. Use a craft knife to cut out the inner circle and discard.

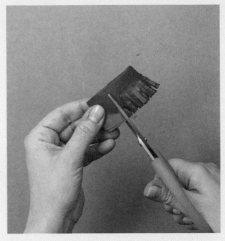

2 Cut two layers of red tissue paper to 20 x 1½ in. (51 x 4 cm). Fold the paper five times along the long edge and, using a strong pair of scissors, make 1-in. (2.5-cm) long parallel cuts to create a fringe.

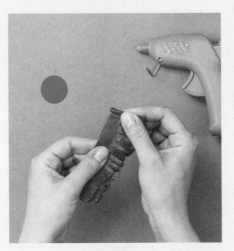

3 Cut a circle of red card 1 in. (2.5 cm) in diameter. Unfold the red tissue paper a couple of times and then start rolling it into a tight spiral.

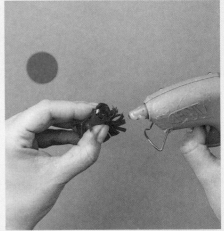

4 Once it is all rolled up, apply hot glue to the base (the end without the fringe) and press it down onto the red card circle to create a small pom-pom flower.

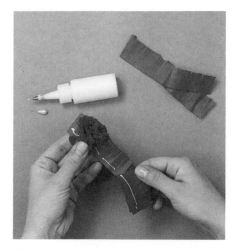

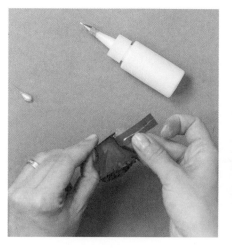

5 To make a larger flower, repeat Step 2 and then roll the fringed tissue paper around the small flower already made. Add as many layers as you want, but remember to make the circle for the base as large as you want the final flower to be.

6 To tidy the flower, trim a thin strip of the tissue paper, approximately 4 in. (10 cm) long. Using PVA glue, stick this to the bottom of the flower, rolling it as close to the base as possible.

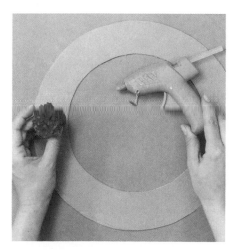

7 Use a dab of hot glue on the base of the flower to attach it to the cardboard ring. (I recommend gluing in place only when you've made all of the pom-poms to ensure an even distribution on the wreath.)

8 Repeat the process to add more pom-pom flowers in different sizes and colors, until the cardboard is covered and your wreath is complete.

TEMPLATES

You'll find the templates mentioned in the projects on the following pages. Remember to use these templates at 100%, except where stated otherwise. It is also a good idea to photocopy the templates so that you can use them over and over again.

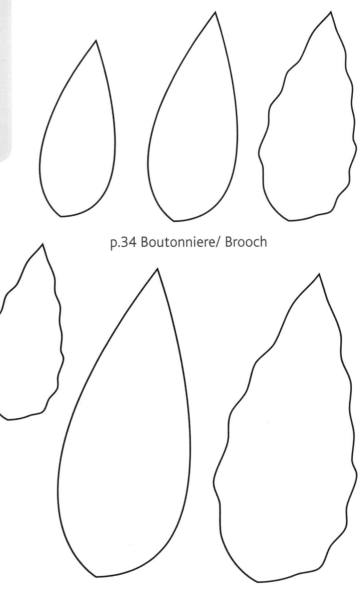

p.34 Boutonniere/ Brooch

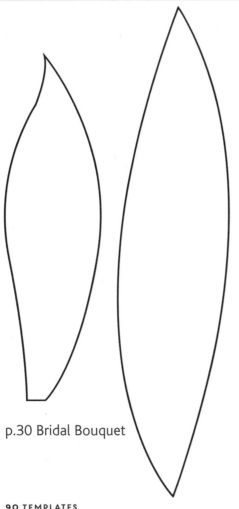

p.30 Bridal Bouquet

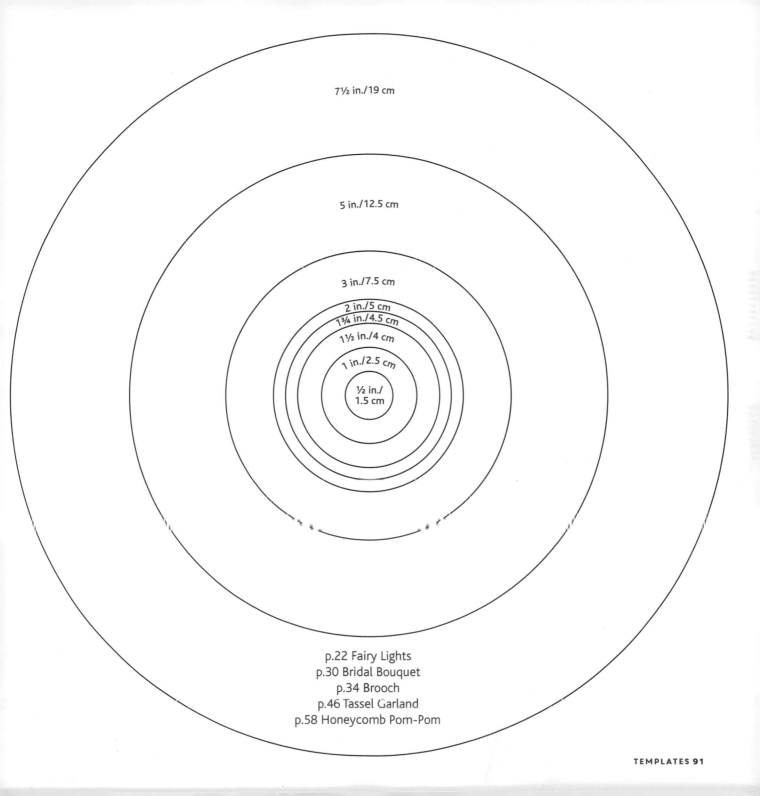

7½ in./19 cm

5 in./12.5 cm

3 in./7.5 cm

2 in./5 cm

1¾ in./4.5 cm

1½ in./4 cm

1 in./2.5 cm

½ in./
1.5 cm

p.22 Fairy Lights
p.30 Bridal Bouquet
p.34 Brooch
p.46 Tassel Garland
p.58 Honeycomb Pom-Pom

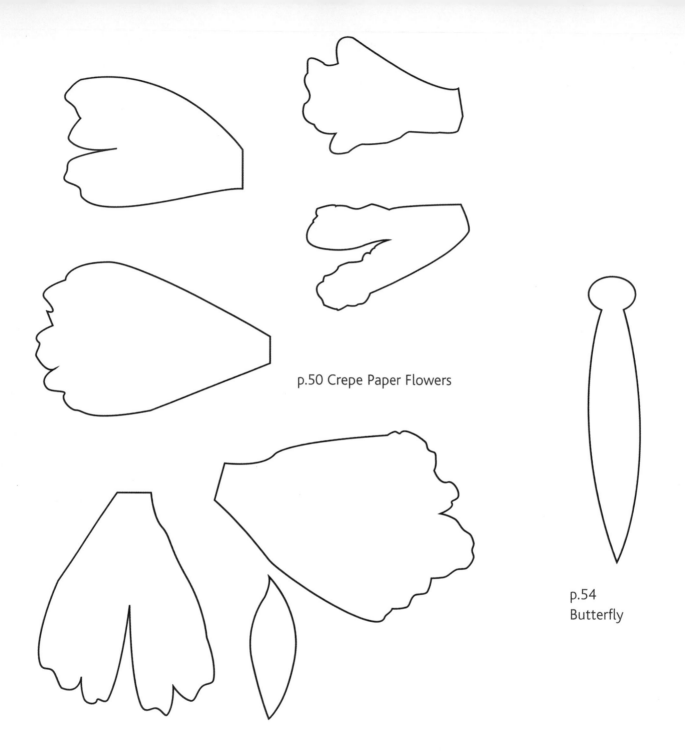

p.50 Crepe Paper Flowers

p.54
Butterfly

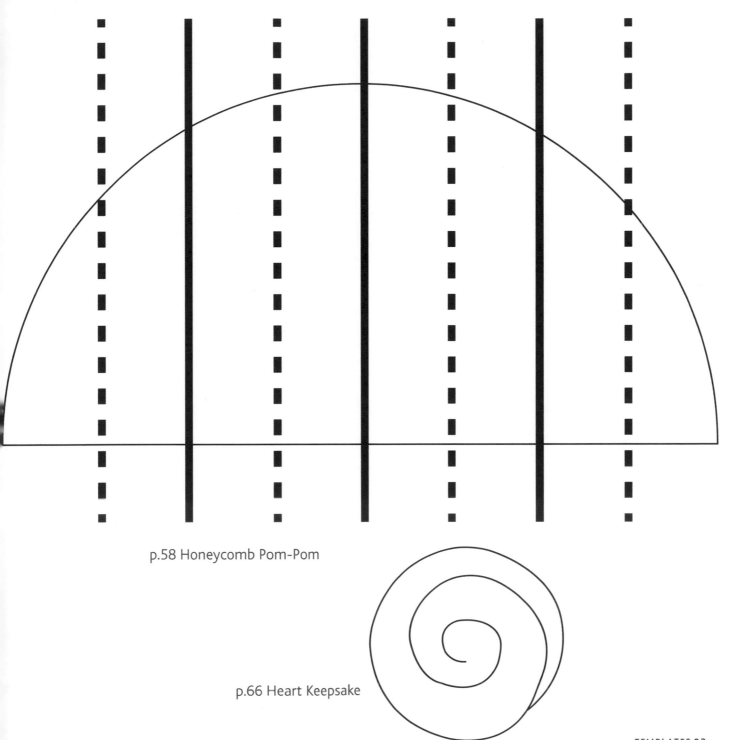

p.58 Honeycomb Pom-Pom

p.66 Heart Keepsake

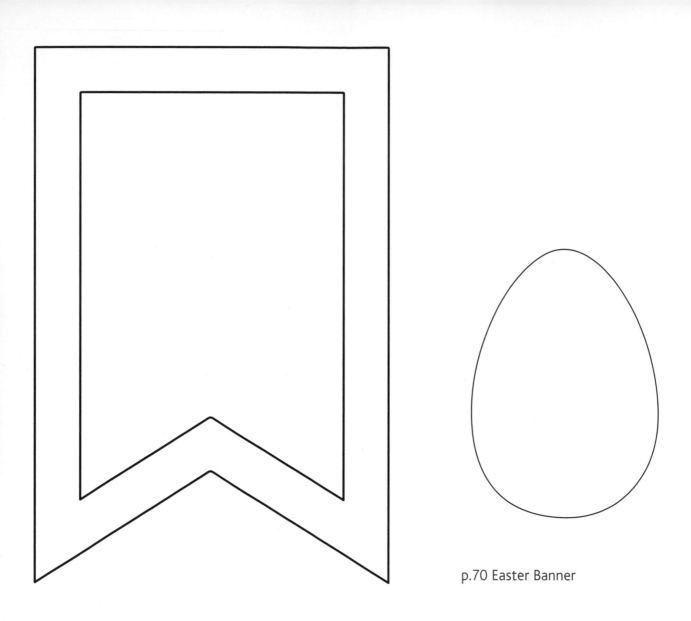

p.70 Easter Banner

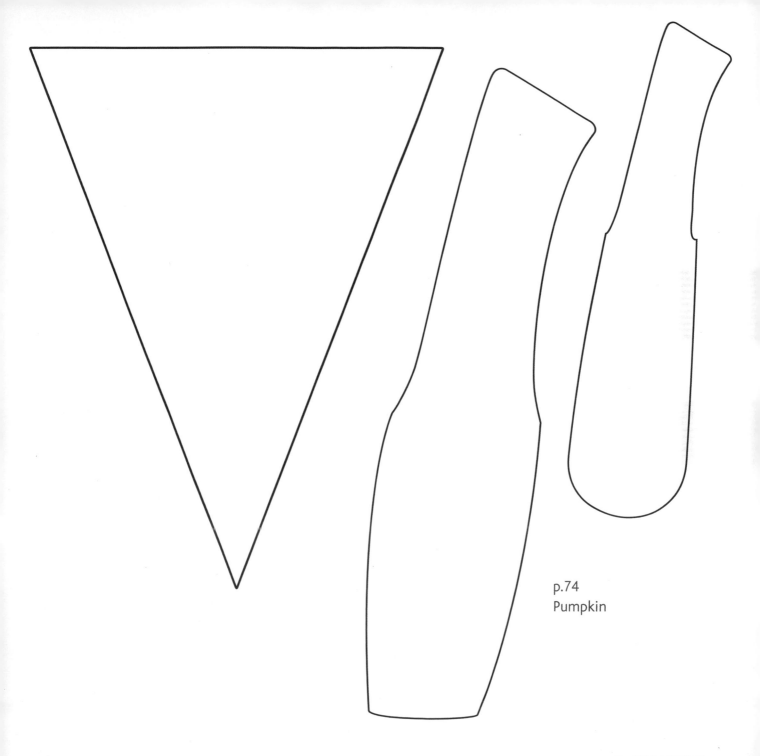

p.74
Pumpkin

Acknowledgments

To my parents Elvira and Angel, from whom I learned the love of beauty, color and paper.

A huge massive thank you to Omar, my very understanding husband for his huge support over the last few months and over the years with my crazy crafting. To my goddaughter, my nieces and nephews for always brightening my day. To my sister Ananda, to my parents, Angela and Javier, to Sarah and Mohsen, thank you for all your faith in me and your relentless support.

To my dearest friends who are always there when I need them, Sephira, Pascal, Nureen, Julie, Patricia, Pete, Lindsay, Marion, Emma, Leandra, Nina, Jo, Fabrizio, Vincent, Quim, Elena, Alberto, all of you have kept my crafty craziness in check, inspiring me and cheering me along the way.

To Kirsty Neale for thinking of me for this project, to Julia Shone for her stellar work with words and being such a pleasure to work with, to Isabel de Cordova for her amazing styling ideas, to Karl for the photography, last but not least, to Lucy, Alison, Clare for making it happen!

I would also like to thank Stix2, Fiskars, Tonic and Sizzix for all the craft tools and materials provided.